Music for Little People

50 Playful Activities for Preschool and Early Elementary School Children

Compiled by
John M. Feierabend

Illustrated by
Gary M. Kramer

BOOSEY & HAWKES

CONTENTS

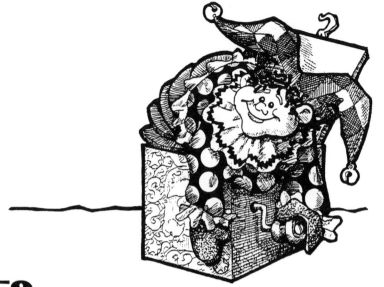

MOVING FINGERS

MOVING BODIES

MOVING TOGETHER

MOVING AROUND

MOVING VOICES

TAKING TURNS

LEADING OTHERS

ACKNOWLEDGEMENTS

Special thanks to Ann C. Kay as well as Mary Beth Ming and her students at the Shepard Boulevard Elementary School in Columbia, Missouri who shared songs that appear in this book. Recognition is here expressed to Andrea Macon and the Children's Chorus of Maryland for participating in the production of the accompanying cassette. Appreciation is also expressed to Sr. Lorna Zemke and Edwin Gordon who enhanced my teaching and my understanding of how children learn. Finally and most importantly I am indebted to my own children Andrew, Charles, and James who have shown me that if given the chance, music can become essential in children's lives far beyond anything I ever thought I was teaching in a music class.

John M. Feierabend   Ph.D.
Collector and Author
Father of three "Little People"
Professor of Music Education
Early Childhood Music Specialist

Gary M. Kramer
Illustrator
Father of two "Little People"
Director, Video Resources Studio
Studio Artist

Luann Saunders
Vocals and Guitar
Mother of two "Little People"
Music Educator
Folksinger

For James and Geoffrey

INTRODUCTION

As children develop from toddlers to preschoolers (around 30 months) their interest in music making becomes more evident. Preschool children love to make music, repeating fragments of familiar songs and developing their own songs. The richer a child's exposure to songs and rhymes, the more imaginative his spontaneous song making can become.

Songs and rhymes in early childhood can be a playful way of enhancing essential developmental skills. They teach concepts, enhance vocabulary, they develop motor skills, and encourage social skills and creative responses. They are happy experiences for children.

Traditional songs and rhymes were selected for this collection for many reasons. They are not contrived. They are singable by young children. They are a natural union of words, rhythm, and melody. They were created by ordinary people out of inspiration. They are living examples of our cultural past. They contain and transmit real human feeling. They are our native musical language. They belong to us.

The other consideration for assembling this collection was to provide activities which would enhance children's abilities to be successful with making music. The path to language ability in early childhood is listening, understanding and the coordination ability necessary to express one's self which progresses from babbling to precision. Music making ability follows a similar course. The motor coordination and vocal coordination necessary to perform songs and rhymes also progresses from "babbling'" to precision.

Songs and rhymes which require less rhythmic precision and are not performed with a consistent pulse are found in "Moving Fingers" and "Moving Bodies". Those activities which encourage the precision of a consistent pulse are in "Moving Together", "Moving Around", and "Leading Others". Awareness of potential vocal ability is the focus of "Moving Voices", while songs which encourage the development of vocal precision are included in "Taking Turns".

TXB-70   Printed in U.S.A.

MOVING FINGERS

The following songs and rhymes include movements which pretend the actions of the words. These activities can be performed while sitting since you will only be using the upper part of your body. When sharing these activities, learn the movements that will be used before you learn the song or the rhyme. If you first learn the movements and then the song or rhyme, you will be better able to combine them. Ready? Can you make your fingers look like this?

1 Help Me Wind My Ball of Wool

Help me wind my ball of wool.

Hold it gen - tly; Do not pull,

Wind the wool and wind the wool, A -

round, a - round, a - round.

2 Chop, Chop, Chippity Chop

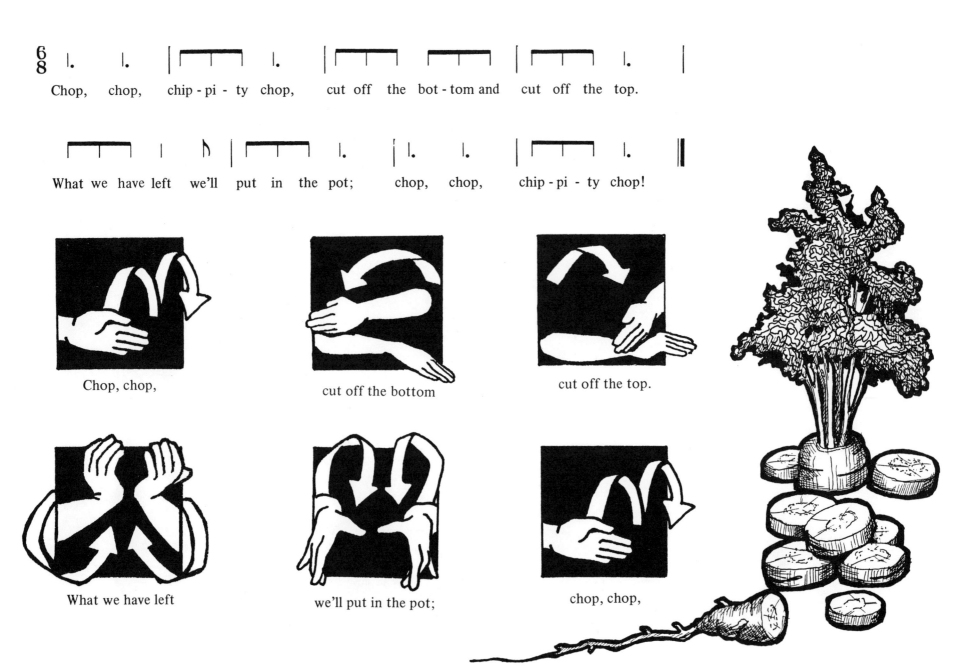

Chop, chop, chip-pi-ty chop, cut off the bot-tom and cut off the top.

What we have left we'll put in the pot; chop, chop, chip-pi-ty chop!

Chop, chop,

cut off the bottom

cut off the top.

What we have left

we'll put in the pot;

chop, chop,

3 Grandma's Glasses

Grandma's glasses,

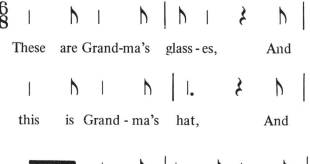

These are Grand-ma's glass-es, And

this is Grand-ma's hat, And

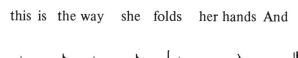

this is the way she folds her hands And

lays them in her lap.

hat

folds her hands

lays them in her lap.

Grandpa's glasses.

hat

folds his arms

Just like that.

Verse 2.

These are Grandpa's glasses,
And this is Grandpa's hat,
And this is the way he folds his arms
Just like that.

10

4 Do Your Ears Hang Low?

Do your ears hang low? Do they

wob-ble to and fro? Can you

tie them in a knot? Can you

tie them in a bow? Can you

throw them o-ver your shoul-der Like a

con-ti-nen-tal sol-dier? Do your

ears hang low?

ears hang low?

wobble to and fro?

tie them in a knot?

tie them in a bow?

over your shoulder

continental soldier?

ears hang low?

5 Five Little Ladies

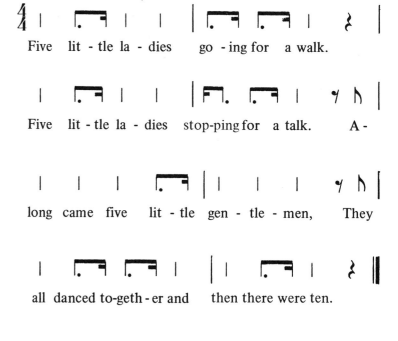

Five lit-tle la-dies go-ing for a walk.

Five lit-tle la-dies stop-ping for a talk. A-

long came five lit-tle gen-tle-men, They

all danced to-geth-er and then there were ten.

going for a walk.

stopping for a talk.

five little gentlemen,

all danced together

6 Eensy Weensy Spider

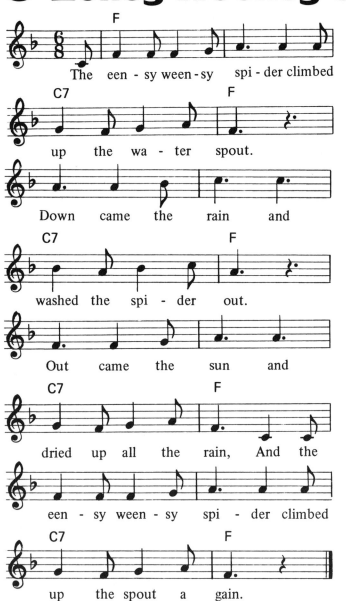

The een-sy ween-sy spi-der climbed up the wa-ter spout. Down came the rain and washed the spi-der out. Out came the sun and dried up all the rain, And the een-sy ween-sy spi-der climbed up the spout a gain.

eensy weensy spider

alternate

up the water spout.

Down came

washed the spider out.

Out came

dried up all the rain,

eensy weensy spider

alternate

up the spout again.

Verse 2: The eensy weensy spider kept climbing up the spout.
He climbed and he climbed while trying to get out;
He kept right on climbing and never did he stop.
And the eensy weensy spider, at last he reached the top.

14

7 Three Little Monkeys

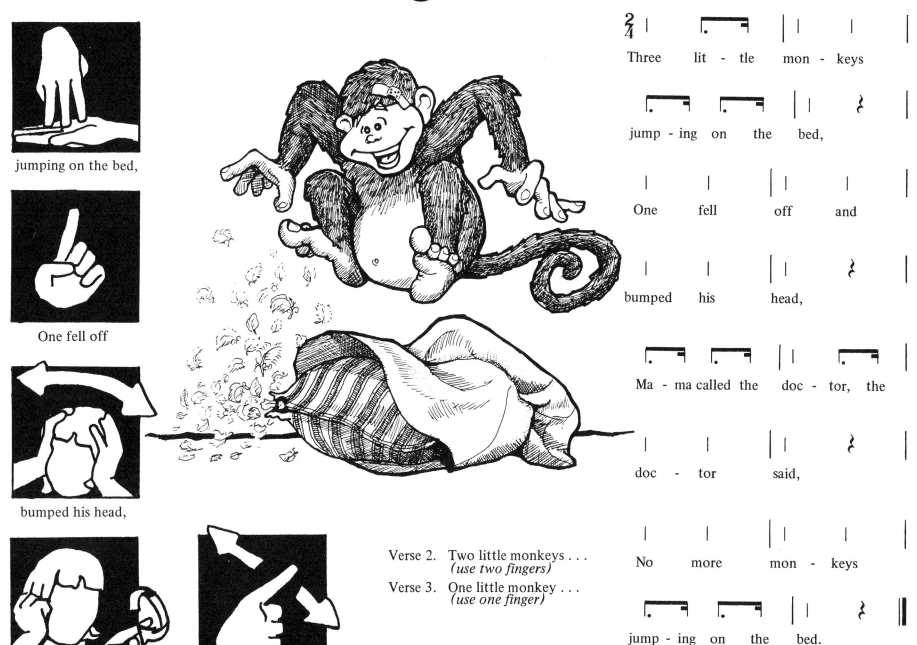

jumping on the bed,

One fell off

bumped his head,

called the doctor,

No more monkeys

Verse 2. Two little monkeys . . .
(use two fingers)

Verse 3. One little monkey . . .
(use one finger)

$\frac{2}{4}$ Three lit - tle mon - keys

jump - ing on the bed,

One fell off and

bumped his head,

Ma - ma called the doc - tor, the

doc - tor said,

No more mon - keys

jump - ing on the bed.

15

8 Miss Polly Had a Dolly

$\begin{smallmatrix}6\\8\end{smallmatrix}$

Miss   Pol - ly had a   dol - ly who was sick, sick,   sick.   She

phoned for the doc - tor to come quick, quick, quick.   The

doc - tor   came with his bag   and his hat.   He

knocked on the door with a   rat   a tat   tat.   He

looked   at   the dol - ly and he shook   his   head.   He

said, "Miss   Pol - ly, put her straight to   bed."   He

wrote   on   a   pa - per for a   pill, pill,   pill. "I'll be

back   in   the morn - ing with the   bill, bill,   bill."

Miss Polly had a dolly

phoned for the doctor

doctor came

knocked on the door

shook his head.

put her straight to bed

wrote on a paper

back in the morning

9 Mr. Lynn

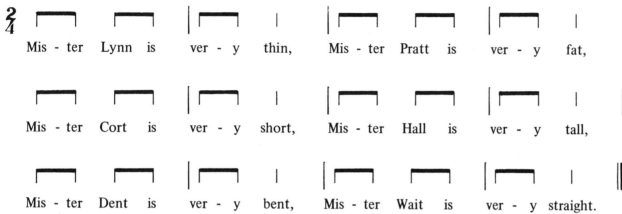

Mis-ter Lynn is ver-y thin, Mis-ter Pratt is ver-y fat,

Mis-ter Cort is ver-y short, Mis-ter Hall is ver-y tall,

Mis-ter Dent is ver-y bent, Mis-ter Wait is ver-y straight.

very thin,

very fat,

very short,

very tall,

very bent,

very straight.

18

10 Five Little Mice

Five lit - tle mice came out to play Gath - er - ing

crumbs a - long the way. Out came the pus - sy - cat sleek and

fat. Four lit - tle mice went scamp - er - ing back.

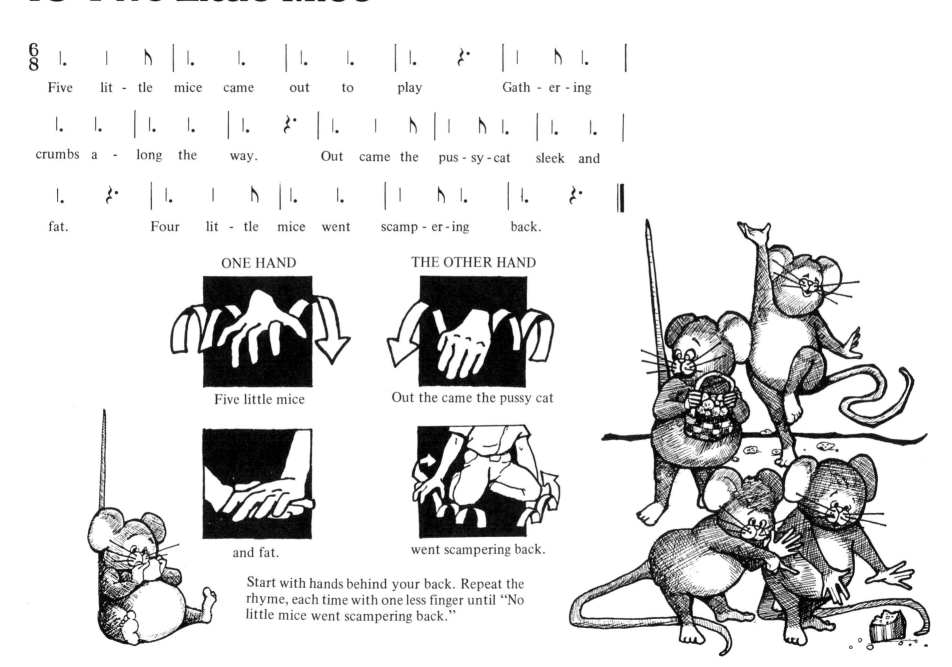

ONE HAND

Five little mice

and fat.

THE OTHER HAND

Out the came the pussy cat

went scampering back.

Start with hands behind your back. Repeat the rhyme, each time with one less finger until "No little mice went scampering back."

19

MOVING BODIES

You will need to be ready to stand up and sit down and maybe stand up again with the following songs and rhymes. We will be moving our whole bodies as we act out the motions of the words. As with the previous section you should learn the movements for each song or rhyme before you add the words and music. Gather your energy. Here we go!

20

11 The Jack-in-the-Box

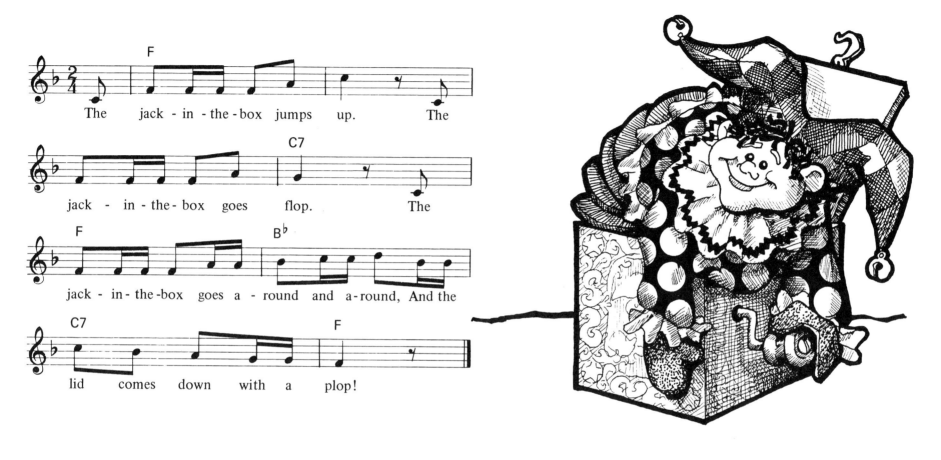

The jack-in-the-box jumps up. The jack-in-the-box goes flop. The jack-in-the-box goes a-round and a-round, And the lid comes down with a plop!

jumps up.

goes flop.

around and around,

down with a plop!

12 Wake Up You Lazy Bones

Wake up

cows are gone.

sun is hot.

I'll rest

'till they come home.

D
Wake up you la - zy bones and

A7   D
go and fetch the cat - tle.

Wake up you la - zy bones and

A7   D   *Fine*
go and fetch the cows.

A7   D
The cows are gone.

A7   D
The sun is hot.

A7   D
I think I'll rest

D. C. al Fine

A7   D
'till they come home.

Shout: "Wake up you lazy bones."

22

13 Cousin Peter

Action Song

Last_ eve - ning cous - in _ Pe - ter came,

Last_ eve - ning cous - in _ Pe - ter came,

Last_ eve - ning cous - in_ Pe - ter came

Just to say that he was here.

Verse 2: He wiped his feet upon the mat (3 times)
Just to show that he was here.

Verse 3: He hung his hat upon the peg (3 times)
Just to show that he was here.

Verse 4: He played he was a great big bear (3 times)
Just to show that he was here.

Verse 5: He picked me up into the air (3 times)
Just to show that he was here.

Verse 6: He made a bow and said said "Goodbye" (3 times)
Just to show that he was here.

cousin Peter came,

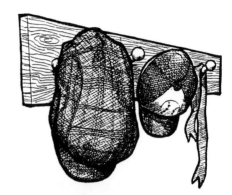

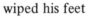

wiped his feet

hung his hat

great big bear

picked me up

made a bow

alternate

said "Goodbye"

24

14 Head and Shoulders, Knees and Toes

Head and shoul-ders, knees and toes, knees and toes, Head and shoul-ders, knees and toes, knees and toes,— My—

eyes and ears and mouth— and— nose, Head and shoul-ders, knees and toes, knees and toes.

Head

shoulders,

knees

toes,

eyes

ears

mouth

nose,

15 The Wheels on the Bus

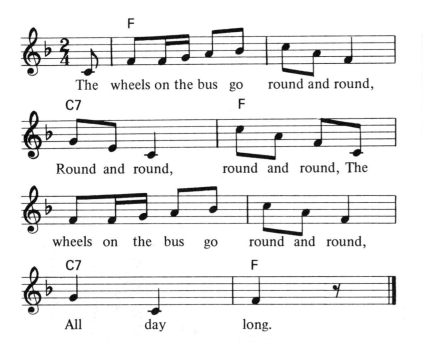

The wheels on the bus go round and round,
Round and round, round and round, The
wheels on the bus go round and round,
All day long.

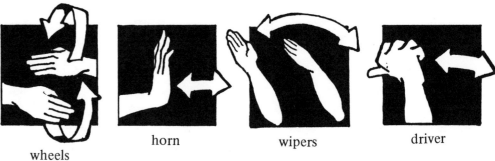

wheels   horn   wipers   driver

people   baby   mother

Verse 2. The horn on the bus goes peep, peep, peep . . .

Verse 3. The wipers on the bus go swish, swish, swish . . .

Verse 4. The driver on the bus says, "Move on back," . . .

Verse 5. The people on the bus bounce up and down . . .

Verse 6. The baby on the bus says, "Wah, wah, wah," . . .

Verse 7. The mother on the bus says, "Sh, sh, sh," . . .

Ride The Bus All Day Long All Over Town

16 The Noble Duke of York

noble Duke

ten thousand men,

top of the hill,

down again;

up

down

Oh, the no - ble Duke of York, He

had ten thou - sand men, He

marched them up to the top of the hill, And he

marched them down a - gain; Oh, and

D.C.

halfway up

of York

ten thousand men,

when you're up you're up; And

when you're down you're down; And

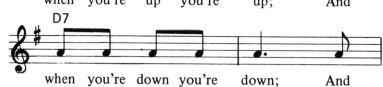

when you're on - ly half - way up you're

D.C. al Fine

half - way to the ground.

28

17 What the Animals Do

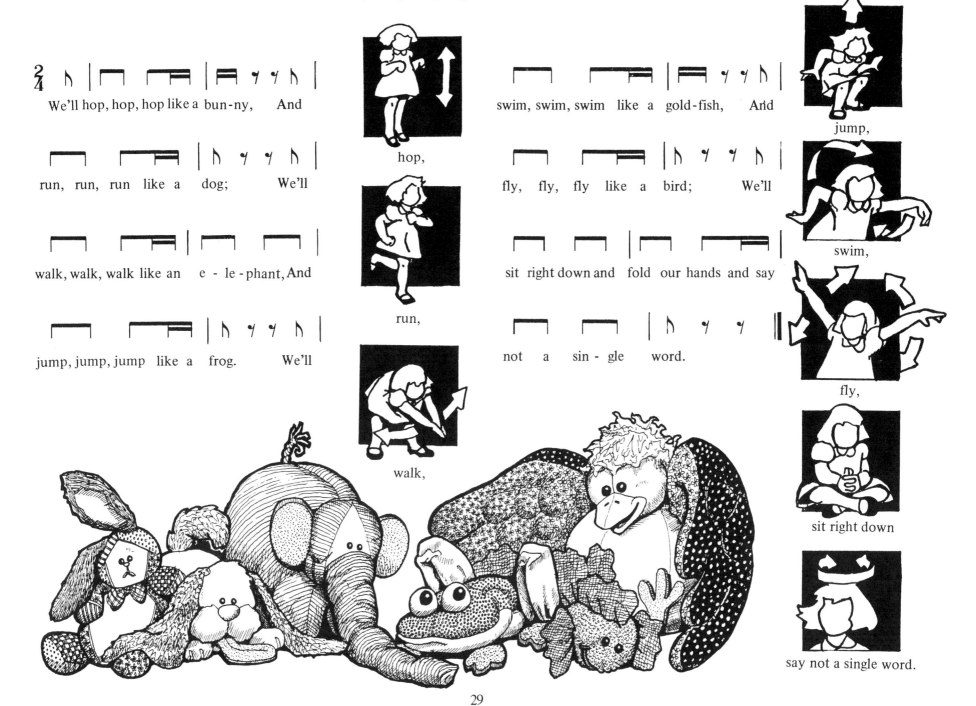

2/4

We'll hop, hop, hop like a bun-ny, And

run, run, run like a dog; We'll

walk, walk, walk like an e-le-phant, And

jump, jump, jump like a frog. We'll

hop,

run,

walk,

swim, swim, swim like a gold-fish, And

fly, fly, fly like a bird; We'll

sit right down and fold our hands and say

not a sin-gle word.

jump,

swim,

fly,

sit right down

say not a single word.

18 The Wiggle Song

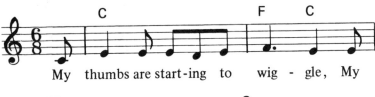

My thumbs are start-ing to wig - gle, My

thumbs are start - ing to wig - gle, My

thumbs are start - ing to wig - gle, A -

round, a - round, a - round.

Verse 2: My thumbs and fingers are wiggling . . .

Verse 3: My hands are starting to wiggle . . .

Verse 4: My arms are starting to wiggle . . .

Verse 5: My head is starting to wiggle . . .

Verse 6: My legs are starting to wiggle . . .

Verse 7: Now all of me is awiggle . . .

thumbs are starting
(Add additional body parts with each verse)

all of me is awiggle

MOVING TOGETHER

Sometimes we can maintain a consistant pulse as we perform some movement with a song or a rhyme. Even though we will be moving by ourselves we will be moving at the same time as each other. Repeat each motion keeping a consistant pulse from the beginning of the song until the end. Can we do our movements together?

 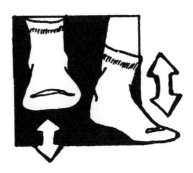 

19 I Can Hammer

I can ham-mer with one ham-mer,

I can ham-mer with one ham-mer,

I can ham-mer with one ham-mer, And

ham-mer and ham-mer all day.

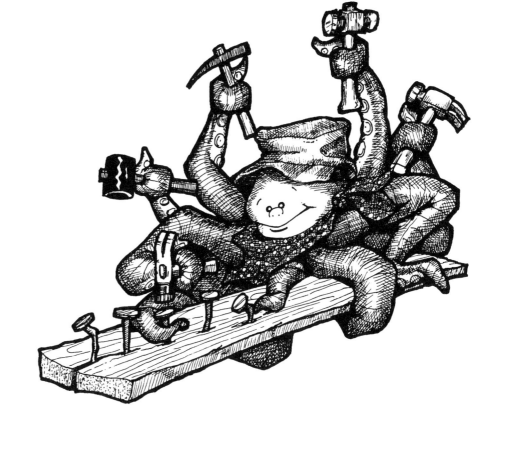

Verse 2: I can hammer with two hammers . . .

Verse 3: I can hammer with three hammers . . .

Verse 4: I can hammer with four hammers . .

Verse 5: I can hammer with five hammers . . .

one hammer,

two hammers

three hammers

four hammers

five hammers

or

five hammers

20 Haul Away Joe!

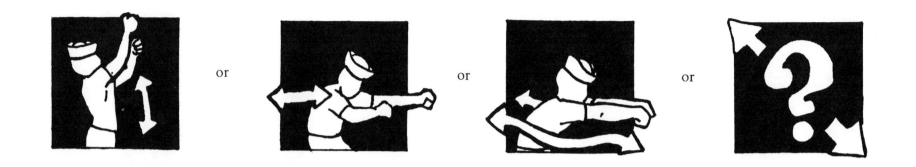

or ... or ... or

Dm ... Am
Way, haul a - way, ___ Oh

Gm ... Am
haul and sing to - geth - er. ___

Dm ... Am
Way, haul a - way. ___ We'll

Gm ... A7 ... Dm
haul a - way Joe!

21 One Finger, One Thumb

One fin-ger, one thumb, keep mov - ing, keep mov - ing, keep mov - ing, One fin - ger, one thumb, keep mov - ing And chase the flies a - way.

 and

One finger, one thumb,

chase the flies away.

Two fingers, two thumbs,

Verse 2: Two fingers, two thumbs, keep moving . . .

Verse 3: Two fingers, two thumbs, two arms, keep moving . . .

Verse 4: Two fingers, two thumbs, two arms, two feet, keep moving . . .

Verse 5: Two fingers, two thumbs, two arms, two feet, stand up, sit down, keep moving . . .

*Extra words inserted here are sung on the same tone as "one thumb".

Two fingers, two thumbs, two arms,

Two fingers, two thumbs, two arms, two feet,

stand up, sit down,

36

22 The Horse Stood Around

Oh, the horse stood a-round with his foot on the ground, Oh, the

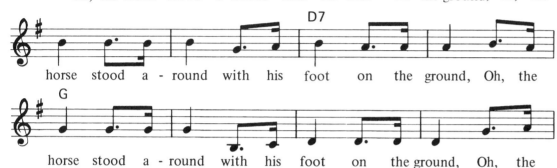

horse stood a-round with his foot on the ground, Oh, the

horse stood a-round with his foot on the ground, Oh, the

horse stood a-round — with his foot on the ground.

Verse 2. *(spoken before repeat)*

Same horse, the o-ther foot.

Verse 3. *(spoken before repeat)*

Same horse, chang-ing feet.

Verse 4. *(spoken before repeat)*

Same horse, both feet.

Verse 5. *(spoken before repeat)*

Same horse, one foot.

horse stood around

the other foot.

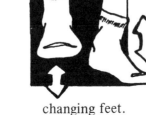

changing feet.

both feet.

one foot.

23 Ali Baba and the Forty Thieves

Leader chants and performs a motion on the beat.
Children repeat chant and motion.

Al - i   Ba - ba and the for - ty thieves

 or  or

Possible motions to perform on the beat with chant.

> tap legs
> tap floor
> clap hands
> tap head
> nod head
> touch nose
> pull ears
> snap fingers

Later:

Leader performs the chant and first motion. While children are repeating the chant with the first motion, the leader is simultaneously performing a second motion. While the children are performing the chant with the second motion, the leader is simultaneously performing a third motion . . . etc. . . . .

Later:

Children sit in a circle, leader performs the first motion. While the first child echos the chant and first motion, the leader is simultaneously performing a second motion. Next, the second child echos the first motion, the first child simultaneously echos the second motion, and the leader simultaneously performs a third motion. This chain is continued until all children are performing different motions simultaneously.

24 Mother Goonie Bird

"Right wing"

"Left wing"

"Right foot"

"Left foot"

"Now your head"

"Sit down"

Verse 2. *"Left wing"*
Verse 3. *"Right foot"*
Verse 4. *"Left foot"*
Verse 5. *"Now your head"*
Verse 6. *"Sit down"*

1. Moth-er Goon-ie Bird had sev-en chicks, sev-en chicks had Moth-er Goon-ie Bird, And they could-n't walk, And they could-n't talk, But they could all go like this. *"Right wing"*

© Copyright John M. Feierabend 1986.

40

25 See How I'm Jumping

See how I'm jump-ing, jump-ing, jump-ing!

See how I'm bounc-ing like a ball.

You did-n't know I could jump so high.

You did-n't know I could stand so still.

See how I'm jump-ing, jump-ing, jump-ing.

When I am tir-ed down I flop.

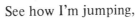   

See how I'm jumping,   stand so still.   See how I'm jumping,   down I flop.

41

MOVING AROUND

Some songs need the help of a few friends. You might find yourself holding hands in a line or sitting in a circle. Together, you will be asked to move or move something around. Move with the same pulse as everyone else and see how much fun moving around can be.

26 Alley-Alley-O

Oh the big ship sail-ing on the al-ley al-ley-o, The
al-ley-al-ley-o, The al-ley-al-ley-o; Oh the big ship sail-ing on the
al-ley-al-ley-o; On the nine-teenth of Sep-tem-ber.

27 Slip One and Two

Slip one and two,

jump three and four,

Turn a - round quick - ly and

sit up - on the floor.

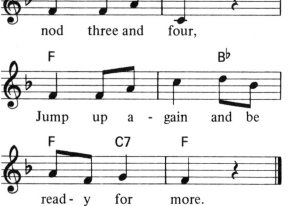

Clap one and two,

nod three and four,

Jump up a - gain and be

read - y for more.

Slip one and two,

jump

Turn around quickly

sit upon the floor.

Clap

nod

Jump up again and
be ready for more.

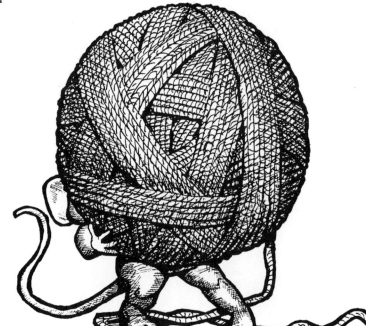

44

28 Wind the Bobbin

Wind the bobbin,

Wind the bob-bin, Ding Dong. Gon-na

Wind it tight, Ding Dong.

Bob-bin a wound up, Bob-bin a wound up,

Bob-bin a wound up. Ding Dong. Gon-na
Last verse: "Break it."

"Break it."

29 Hey Betty Martin

Chorus:

F

Hey Bet-ty Mar-tin, tip-py toe, tip-py toe,

Hey Bet-ty Mar-tin tip-toe-fine.   C7

F

Hey Bet-ty Mar-tin, tip-py toe, tip-py toe,

C7   F   *Fine*

Hey Bet-ty Mar-tin tip-toe fine.

Verse:

C7   F

Jump with me, I'll jump with you;

C7   F

We'll go jump-ing the whole day through.

C7   F

Jump so fine, jump so fine,

G7   C   *D. C. al Fine*

Jump-ing, jump-ing all the time.

tippy toe,

Jump with me,   or

30 Pass the Shoe

F

I pass the shoe from me to you, to you, I
* **

C7   F

pass the shoe and this is what I do.
*   *

Early: While group sits on the floor in a circle, pass the shoe.
Each individual should set the shoe down on the beat,
in front of the person sitting next to him.

Later: While group sits on the floor in a circle, each child re-
moves one shoe. All children pass a shoe on each beat.

** Try passing other objects such as a cup (paper or styrofoam), bean bag, or stuffed animal.
* Pass.

31 Old King Glory

F

Old King Glo-ry on the moun - tain, The

C7

moun-tain was so high, It near - ly touched the sky. The

F

first one, the sec - ond one, the third one fol - low me.

Old King Glory

third one follow me.

32 Circle 'Round the Zero

Circle 'round

Back, back,

D

Cir - cle 'round the ze - ro,

Find your lov - in' ze - ro.

Back, back, ze - ro,

Side, side, ze - ro.

Front, front, ze - ro.

Tap your lov - in' ze - ro.

Side, side,

Front, front,

Tap your lovin' zero.

51

MOVING VOICES

There are lots of interesting sounds we can make with our voices: animal sounds, yodels, and sirens to name a few. Here are two stories which need your help. The first needs a hum of delight and the second one needs a cowboy call. Can you help tell these stories by moving your voice?

33 The Ice Cream Sundae

John M. Feierabend

Today was a day I did everything right,
Though my brother annoyed me I still didn't fight.
I played nicely all day, didn't argue or scream,
Now my mom says we'll go for a dish of ice cream. (mmmm)

I ate all of my breakfast and all of my lunch,
I picked up my toys (and I have a bunch),
And since I've been helpful, like part of a team,
I think I might ask for two scoops of ice cream. (mmmm)

Two scoops! What a treat! But I think you'll agree,
It would be hard to imagine one better than me.
I've done everything right or so it would seem,
Maybe Mom will allow me four scoops of ice cream. (mmmm)

Yes! Today has been special. It's not every day,
I do everything right in such a nice way.
So why not, of course, since I'm building up steam,
Have some syrup on top of four scoops of ice cream. (mmmm)

"You've been perfect young man." That's what Mom said today,
So I know she won't mind if I have it my way.
To the syrup add nuts and also whipped cream,
And a cherry on top of four scoops of ice cream. (mmmm)

And yet when I think about wanting more,
Though it sounds awfully good, I know what's in store.
I'll eat and I'll eat then . . . I'll run out of steam,
And I won't feel so good after all that ice cream. (mmmm)

Since today was a day I did everything right,
I will not spoil my record by making a sight,
I'll ask most politely (though it was fun to dream),
"May I have one scoop of vanilla ice cream?" (mmmm)

53

34 The Ballad of Cowboy Joe

John M. Feierabend

Cowboy Joe was a bold young man.
He dreamed of rustling cattle most of all.
He wanted to see if the cows would come
When he let out his cowboy call. (yee—haa)

He practiced all day from morning to night,
And he practiced both summer and fall.
He knew some day he'd have his chance
To try out his cowboy call. (yee—haa)

Well finally one day it was proudly announced
That his ma and pa and all,
Were takin' trip to his grandfather's ranch
Where he could try out his cowboy call. (yee—haa)

He jumped for joy and ran for his gear
And ran back down the hall.
He hopped in the car and was ready to go
To let out his cowboy call. (yee—haa)

When they arrived at the ranch he was happy to see
That the cows were not in the stall.
He dashed to the field where they quietly grazed
And he let out his cowboy call. (yee—haa)

Well they all did come right up to the fence
And he sure felt ten feet tall.
"I'm Cowboy Joe. See how the cows come
When I let out my cowboy call?" (yee—haa)

Now that was really some day for Cowboy Joe
And he sure did have a ball.
Now he's wantin' to try bigger and better things
So he's practicing his elephant call. (?)

TAKING TURNS

Some songs have a part for me and a part for you. These are songs in which we will take turns singing. After you learn these songs you can sing the first parts and have a friend sing after you. Listen! It's my turn –––––– your turn ––––––

35 Oh, My! No More Pie

Oh, my!_ oh, my!_

No more pie.*
Pie's too sweet,
I wanna piece of meat.
Meat's too red,
I wanna piece of bread.
Bread's too brown,
I think I'll go to town.
Town's too far,

I think I'll take a car.
Car won't go.
I fell and stubbed my toe.
Toe gives me pain,
I think I'll take a train.
Train had a wreck,
I fell and broke my neck.
Oh, my!
No more pie.

*Echo each phrase.

Oh, my!

Oh, my!

36 Bill Grogan's Goat

Leader: Echo:

1. There was a man, There was a man,

Now please take note, Now please take note,

There was a man, There was a man,

Who had a goat, Who had a goat,

He loved that goat, He loved that goat,

In-deed he did, In-deed he did,

He loved that goat, He loved that goat,

Just like a kid, Just like a kid.

2. One day that goat*
   Felt frisk and fine.
   Ate three red shirts
   Right off the line.
   The man, he grabbed
   Him by the back
   And tied him to
   The railroad track.

3. Now when that train
   Came into sight
   That goat grew pale
   And green with fright.
   He heaved a sigh
   As if in pain,
   Coughed up those shirts
   And flagged the train.

*Echo each phrase.

There was a man,

There was a man,

58

37 The Bear Song

Leader: Echo:

C

1. The oth-er day, The oth-er day,

I met a bear, I met a bear,

G7

Out in the woods, Out in the woods,

C

A-way out there, A-way out there,

All sing:

The oth-er day I met a

F   G7

bear, _____ Out in the woods a -

C

way out there. _____

2. I looked at him,* he looked at me
   I sized up him, he sized up me,

3. He said to me, "Why don't you run,
   I see you ain't got any gun."

4. I said to him, "That's a good idea,"
   So come on feet, let's up and fleet!

5. And so I ran, away from there
   But right behind me was that bear.

6. Oh what do I see ahead of me,
   A great big tree, Oh glory be.

7. The lowest branch was ten feet up,
   I'd have to jump and trust my luck.

8. And so I jumped into the air,
   But I missed that branch away up there.

9. Now don't you fret, and don't you frown,
   'Cause I caught that branch on the way back down.

10. This is the end, there is no more,
    Unless I see that bear once more.

*Echo each phrase.

The other day,

The other day,

(All sing)

38 Oh, In the Woods

Leader: F   Echo:

1. Oh, in the woods, Oh, in the woods,

There was a tree, There was a tree,

The pret-ti-est lit-tle tree, The pret-ti-est lit-tle tree,

C7

That you ev-er did see. That you ev-er did see.

All sing:*   F   C7

The tree was in the hole, And the

F   C7   F   C7

hole was in the ground, And the green grass grew all a-

F   Bb   F   C7   F

round, and a-round, And the green grass grew all a-round.

*Repeat as needed for each additional verse.

2. Now on that tree*
   There was a branch,
   The prettiest little branch
   That you ever did see.

All: The branch was on the tree,
And the tree was in the hole,
And the hole was in the ground,
And the green grass grew all around, and around,
And the green grass grew all around.

3. Now on that branch . . . there was a nest, etc.
4. Now on that nest . . . there was an egg, etc.
5. Now on that egg . . . there was a bird, etc.
6. Now on that bird . . . there was a wing, etc.
7. Now on that wing . . . there was a bug, etc.
8. Now on that bug . . . there was a germ, etc.

*Echo each phrase.

Oh, in the woods,

Oh, in the woods,

(All sing)

39 John the Rabbit

Oh, John the rabbit,

Oh, yes,

40 Oh, My Aunt Came Back

Leader: F   Echo

1. Oh, my aunt came back, Oh, my aunt came back,

C7

From Tim - buk - tu, From Tim - buk - tu,

She brought with her, She brought with her,

F

A wood - en shoe, A wood - en shoe.
      *   *   *   *

*(tap toe)

Oh, my aunt came back,

Oh, my aunt came back,

(continue tapping throughout)

2. Oh, my aunt came back*
   From old Japan.
   She brought with her
   A waving fan.
   (continue tapping and fanning throughout)

3. Oh, my aunt came back
   From old Algiers.
   She brought with her
   A pair of shears.
   (continue tapping, fanning and snipping throughout)

4. Oh, my aunt came back
   From Guadeloupe.
   She brought with her
   A hula hoop.
   (continue tapping, fanning, snipping and hulaing throughout)

5. Oh, my aunt came back
   From the County Fair.
   She brought with her
   A rocking chair.
   (continue tapping, fanning, snipping, hulaing and rocking throughout)

6. Oh, my aunt came back
   From the City Zoo.
   She brought with her
   A nut like you!
   (stop all motions—hands on hips)

*Echo each phrase.

wooden shoe.

waving fan.

pair of shears.

hula hoop.

rocking chair.

nut like you!

41 Down by the Bay

Leader: Echo:

Down by the bay, Down by the bay,

Where the wa-ter-me-lons grow, Where the wa-ter-mel-ons grow,

Back to my home, Back to my home,

I dare not go, I dare not go,

For if I do, For if I do,

My moth-er will say, My moth-er will say,

Leader or Solo:

Verse 1. "Did you ev-er see a bear

All sing:

comb-ing his hair?" Down by the bay.

Down by the bay,

Down by the bay,

"Did you ever see

2. "Did you ever see a bee
   With a sunburned knee?" . . .

3. "Did you ever see a moose
   Kissing a goose?" . . .

4. "Did you ever see a whale
   With a polkadot tail?" . . .

5. "Did you ever see a fly
   Wearing a tie?" . . .

65

42 Oh, You Can't Get to Heaven

2. Oh, you can't get to heaven*
   In a rocking chair . . .
   'Cause the Lord don't want . . .
   No lazy bones there . . .

All: Oh you can't get to heaven in a rocking chair,
   'Cause the Lord don't want no lazy bones there,
   Oh I ain't a gonna grieve my Lord no more.
   Oh I ain't a gonna grieve my Lord no more,
   Oh I ain't a gonna grieve my Lord no more,
   Oh I ain't a gonna grieve my Lord no more.

3. Oh, you can't get to heaven . . .
   In a limousine . . .
   'Cause the Lord don't sell . . .
   No gasoline . . .

All: Oh, you can't get to heaven . . . (etc.)

4. Oh, you can't get to heaven . . .
   In a motor car . . .
   'Cause a motor car . . .
   Won't go that far . . .

All: Oh, you can't get to heaven . . . (etc.)

Oh, you can't get

5. Oh, you can't get to heaven . . .
   In a birch canoe . . .
   You'll need to paddle . . .
   'Till you're black and blue . . .

All: Oh, you can't get to heaven . . . (etc.)

Oh, you can't get

6. If you get to heaven . . .
   Before I do . . .
   Just bore a hole . . .
   And pull me through . . .

All: If you get to heaven . . . (etc.)

(All sing)

*Echo each phrase.

66

LEADING OTHERS

Most of us enjoy becoming a leader once in a while. Here are some songs in which we will take turns leading each other with our favorite repeated movement. Make sure your repeated movement has a consistant pulse so it will be easy to follow. When following another leader imitate his movement and his pulse. Ready? Do this.

43 Dame Get Up

Dame get up___ and bake your pies,

Bake your pies, Bake your pies,

Dame get up___ and bake your pies on

this fine day in the morn - ing.

or

44 Puncinella

Now look who is here, Pun – ci – nel – la, Pun – ci – nel – la,

Look who is here, Pun – ci – nel – la in the shoe.

look who is here,

what can you do

or

Verse 2. Now what can you do
Puncinella, Puncinella . . .

Verse 3. Now we can do it too
Puncinella, Puncinella . . .

Verse 4. Now who do you choose
Puncinella, Puncinella . . .

we can do it too

who do you choose

70

45 The Monkey Stomps

The mon-key stomps, stomps, stomps his feet, The
mon-key stomps, stomps, stomps his feet.
Mon-key see; mon-key do; The
mon-key does the same as you.

46 Francisco

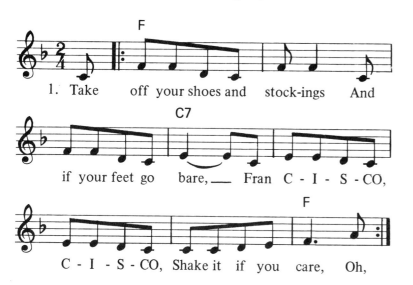

1. Take off your shoes and stock-ings And if your feet go bare, — Fran C - I - S - CO, C - I - S - CO, Shake it if you care, Oh,

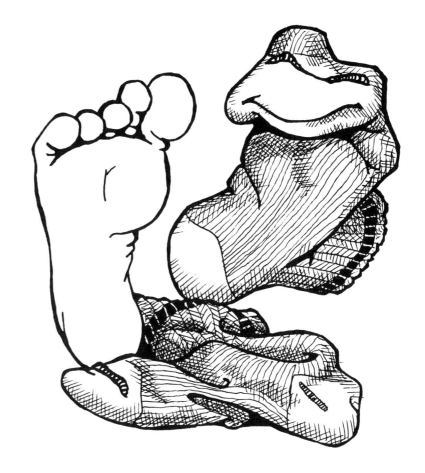

2. Shake it baby, shake it.
   Shake it if you care.
   Fran - C - I - S - CO, C - I - S - CO.
   Shake it if you care, Oh!

3. Tumble to the bottom,
   Tumble to the top.
   Turn yourself around and around
   And then you have to STOP!

Take off your shoes and stockings

Shake it baby,

or

Tumble to the bottom,

47 My Mother Sent Me Unto You

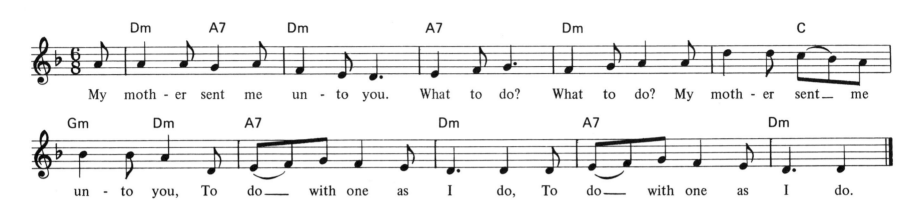

My moth-er sent me un-to you. What to do? What to do? My moth-er sent__ me un-to you, To do__ with one as I do, To do__ with one as I do.

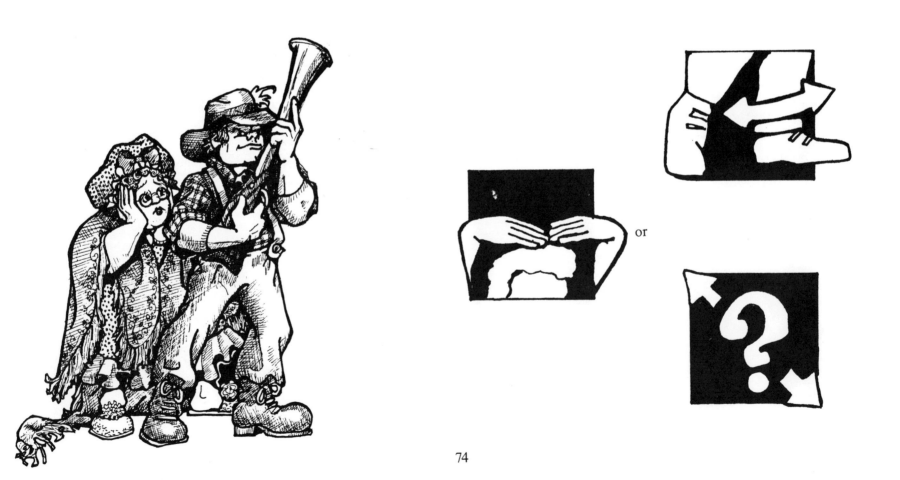

or

48 Dayenu

We are march-ing out of E - gypt, Fol-low-ing our no - ble lead - er,

March-ing proud-ly, sing-ing loud-ly, Da - ye - nu. Da - da - ye - nu, —

Da - da - ye - nu, — Da - da - ye - nu, Da - ye - nu, Da-ye - nu. —

We are marching

or

Da - da - ye - nu,

49 William Had Seven Sons

Dm   Gm   Dm

Wil-liam had __ sev - en sons,   sev - en sons,   sev - en sons,

                              A7   Dm

Wil-liam had __ sev - en sons and   this is   what they   did.

or

or

50 Ambos a Dos

Ambos a dos,

What will you do,

Now we can do it too,

or

Am - bos a dos, ma-ta- ri -le, ri -le, ri -le, Am -

bos a dos, ma-ta - ri -le, ri - le, ron.

Now who do you choose,

2. What will you do, matarile, rile, rile,
   What will you do, matarile, rile, ron?

3. Now we can do it too, matarile, rile, rile,
   Now we can do it too, matarile, rile, ron.

4. Now who do you choose, matarile, rile, rile,
   Now who do you choose, matarile, rile, ron?

78

ALPHABETICAL LISTING

SUBJECT INDEX

ABOUT ME AND MY BODY

ABOUT OTHER PEOPLE

ABOUT OTHER LIVING THINGS

ABOUT THINGS TO EAT

ABOUT GETTING THERE